Field Hockey Penalty corner Push-in - A Biomechanical Approach

Dr. Viswanath Sundar

Lulu Publication
2019

Price: 300/-

**Field Hockey Penalty corner Push-in –
A Biomechanical Approach**

Dr. Viswanath Sundar

© 2019 by Laxmi Book Publication, Solapur.

ISBN– 978-0-359-59985-1

Published by,
Lulu Publication
3101 Hillsborough St,
Raleigh, NC 27607,
United States.

Printed by,
Laxmi Book Publication,
258/34, Raviwar Peth,
Solapur, Maharashtra, India.
Contact No. : 9595359435
Website: http://www.lbp.world
Email ID: apiguide2014@gmail.com

CONTENTS

CHAPTER - I

INTRODUCTION

➤❘❖———————————————❖❘◀

A sport is played for much more than just playing for the sake of play. The sports activity builds up strong manpower, develop mutual trust, co-operation, solidarity and friendship among individuals, teams and nations. The field of sports is currently undergoing remarkable scientific changes and researches have revamped the whole concept of sports. Highly technological innovations through contributions from diverse fields like medicine, engineering, human biology, human performance etcetera, have made the sports field more authentic and interesting. Technological progress during the last century is the result of advancement in mathematics, physics and other applied sciences. Sport activity is not an exception in this respect since sports sciences have been recognized considerably as an academic discipline of study in recent years.

Nowadays, the nature of sports and games has gone through tremendous radical changes in international arena, due to advancement of sports sciences. The sports sciences namely sports psychology, exercise physiology, sports training, sports biomechanics, kinanthropometry and other branches of sports sciences help to enhance performance in a big way at a higher level. Biomechanics one of the branches of sports sciences, is the study of the mechanics of living things. It demands knowledge of both biology and various branches of physics and engineering which comprises mechanics. Kinanthropometry, another sports science subject which has been defined as the quantitative measurement and analysis of age, body, size, shape, proportion, composition and maturation as they relate to gross body function. Modern hockey demands the high perfection of technical skills. The penalty corner is one of the most important game situations with one third of goals resulting from this tactical situation. Biomechanical and kinanthropometric are the major decisive factors which have been neglected by the Indian researchers.

FIELD HOCKEY

Hockey is a dynamic game played by both sexes requiring high level of skills, excellent conditioning and well co-ordinated team effort (Wein, 1981).

Hockey, a sport which emerged in the 19th century, has seen huge changes in the later part of the 20th century and even more changes can be expected as the days go by. "Changes will be, through more of evolution than revolution and that is how it should be". "Hockey is a gentleman's game to be played for its own sake".

ANCESTRY AND DEVELOPMENT OF HOCKEY

There is no definite origin of the game but still a beginning has to be made to the primitive instincts of man hitting an object with something. About 5000 years ago, the people of Persia is known to have played from horseback a game like polo. Historical records show that a rudimentary of the game was played in Egypt 4000 years ago and in Ethiopia around 100 B.C. It was the only game practiced by the Greeks in the epoch of Themistocles (525-449 B.C.). The ancient Aztecs (Mexican Tribe) of South America and the Red Indian Tribes of North America played a savage stick and ball game several centuries before Columbus discovered the new world.

There is also another version that the archeologists have found 4000 year old sketches of men playing what looks to be an early version of hockey in the valley of Egypt. Similar ball and stick games have been linked to the ancient Greeks. There is no indication of synthetic surfaces, mouth guards, shin pads or complex corner plays, but these primitive games were certainly forerunners of day's sport, although modern field hockey evolved in Great Britain in the late 1800s.

HOCKEY IN INDIA

It is one of the greatest records in sports between 1928 and 1964, the Indian men's hockey team lost only one match at Olympic games, winning eight gold medals and one silver. India had an unbeaten sequence of Olympic men's hockey gold medals from 1928 to 1956 and returned with gold medals in 1964 and 1980.

Indeed, it was a great disappointment after India had been disqualified for the Olympics in the year 2012. The question that continues to haunt the hundred crores of people in the subcontinent is that whether it is possible for us to attain the past glory. The crisis management in the wake of frequent losses in Olympics and other International Hockey Tournaments after 1980 is understandable. As a result the administration, coaches, scientists and other observers have studied a lot through analysis. However, depth analysis is required for determining the real cause of defeat in international competitions.

Biomechanical analysis has assumed an important role in competitive sports in the last few decades. The biomechanical analysis based on physical, technical and tactical aspects of the team could enable the coach and the trainers to understand the genesis of biomechanical structure of the team. And thus penalty corner plays a major role in the winning strategy and it is one of the decisive factors which has been neglected by the Indian researchers (Hussain et al., 2011).

SKILLS IN THE GAME OF HOCKEY

Skill is the outcome of message sent by the sensory organs to the brain which in turn makes the concerned muscles act in a certain way to perform a complicated action in the desired manner. In general, a skill is learnt by repeatedly making attempts at movements in such a way that particular muscles are forced to act in certain directions until the requisite skill is acquired.

Hockey players therefore must understand that to get good results they should first grasp the intricacies involved in a skill. They must make up in their mind to create a clear picture of

3

what they are going to attempt. If their mind grasps the whole movement involved in a skill, their tasks in acquiring that skill will become easier. In hockey, the term skill is applied to a pattern of movements which a player is able to make with his stick and ball in a manner that corresponds to rules and is effective in its objective. Hockey is played at a fast pace and a player must use his skills in a manner which corresponds to the tempo of the game. A player who is in the act of stopping or receiving the ball should decide whether his next move is to be a forward pass or a dribble past an opponent.

ORIGIN AND DEVELOPMENT OF PENALTY CORNER

The penalty corner was introduced in 1908 for offences by defenders in their circle. At a penalty corner, the rules require the ball to be stopped before a shot at goal but this was not strictly insisted by umpires. All defenders were behind the goal-line with attacking players outside the circle.

In 1949 deliberate offences by defenders within the 25 yards area and persistent offences by defenders at corners were penalized by a penalty corner.

From 1961, at penalty corners and for long corners, a maximum of six defenders were to be behind the goal line with the remaining of the defending team at the 25 yards line.

In 1975 with the publication of the first common rule book for men and women further changes were made. The ball now had to be stopped dead by an attacker before a shot at goal; there was to be no latitude.

In 1987 saw a further reduction in the number of defenders behind the goal line from six to five. This year also saw the introduction of a height limit on the first hit at goal, the ball should not cross the goal-line higher than 18 inches and if the ball travelled more than 5 yards outside the circle then the penalty corner rules no longer applied.

In 1995, following the introduction of rolling substitutes a few years previously, substitution was now allowed at penalty corners and penalty strokes. This led to the introduction of true specialists, brought on just for penalty corners.

4

In 1996 the stop was moved to outside the circle

From 1997 the rules required the prolongation of play to permit the completion of a penalty corner at half-time and full-time.

From 1998 substitutions at penalty corners were no longer permitted except for an injured defending goalkeeper but were still permitted at penalty strokes.

From 2003 the requirement to stop the ball was removed; instead, the ball was only required to travel outside the circle.

ROLE OF PENALTY CORNER IN FIELD HOCKEY

In modern hockey, there is increase in the number of set plays performed during the game (Patrick, 1997). The penalty corner is one of the most important tactical situations in the field of hockey (Laird & Sutherland, 2003; Pineiro, 2008). The Penalty Corner was introduced in 1908. Penalty corner is awarded for foul committed by the defending team in its own entire 23 meters area. Depending upon the nature of foul, penalty corner is awarded. With penalty corner one has greater scoring opportunities, because at time of start of penalty corner only five defenders will be permitted within the circle but all the attackers are permitted to stand outside the circle. The champions of today are seen perfect in the conversion of penalty corners. It is seen that different variations in penalty corner are being adopted and executed successfully. This requires lot of understanding among the specialized players (Viswanath & Kalidasan, 2012).

When a penalty corner is awarded, all the five defending players (including the goalkeeper) must stay behind the goal line, while the six remaining defenders have to stay behind the centre line. The attacking team players place themselves around the circle with one player behind the back line with the ball. When he pushes out the ball to his team-mates, the defending players may then step inside the field. Before a shot on goal can be taken, the ball must first travel outside the circle. If the ball is hit, other than a flick, scoop or push, the ball must be below 460 mm before crossing the line to score a goal. If the ball raises above 460 mm in its flight, provided there is no danger (If there was it would result in a free hit to the defenders), and drops below 460 mm under its own accord before crossing the goal line (with no interference from the goalkeeper or defenders), it is still counted as a goal.

IMPORTANCE OF PENALTY CORNER

The penalty corner in hockey is one of the most thrilling and controversial part of the game. It changes as its complex rules have conspired to breed a host of specialists who have turned it into key drama. The aim of the penalty corner in attack is to score. In defense it is to prevent a goal either directly or indirectly, in follow -up play.

Penalty corner is one of the most important game situations in field hockey with one third of goals resulting from this tactical situation (Lopez et al., 2011).

PENALTY CORNER PUSH-IN

Penalty corner execution can be separated into three progressive phases: the push- in, the trap and the strike (Wein, 1985). The push-in starts with an attacker standing close to the goal line with at least one foot outside the field of play. The left shoulder points in the direction of the push. The hook of the stick rests against the ball. The push-in movement involves a rapid rotation of the hip, shoulders and arms in the direction of the trapper while the body weight is being transferred from the back foot to the front foot. The ball is dragged or pushed over the playing surface by the hockey stick for some distance and then released in the direction of the trapper. The trap phase follows when the ball reaches the top of the circle and is trapped by another attacking player (the trapper). The trapper then propels the ball back into the circle for phase three to commence. Phase three consists of a third attacker striking the moving ball towards the goal or another attacking player. Although the entire penalty corner takes about 1.9 seconds and 2.3 seconds respectively for male and female players of national standard (Chivers & Elliott, 1987), it is essential that it is performed precisely as it offers an excellent scoring opportunity during the game (Kerr & Ness, 2006).

SPORTS SCIENCES

The performance of the team wholly depends on the proficiency of the skill of each individual. The coaches need to work continuously to enhance the level of efficiency in the performance of the skills of his players. A scientific knowledge about these skills is inevitable on the part of the coaches and scientist to enhance the performance of the skills in the players. The coaches and scientists must analyse each skill and train in order to make the players deliver maximum performance with minimum effort. Sports science plays major role in analysing the skill performance of the player such as test and measurement to identify the current status of a player, sport training to improve the motor qualities of a player, sports biomechanics to channelize the skills of the player with minimum effort and minimal injury and kinanthropometry is to identify the right body composition for the right sport. Among all the sports sciences, sports biomechanics and kinanthropometry play a pivotal role in the enhancement of the skill performance of the player.

SPORTS BIOMECHANICS

McGinnis (2005) Sports Biomechanics is defined as the study of forces and their effects on humans in sport and exercise.

Biomechanics involves the synthesis of many scientific disciplines such as work and energy in Physics, forces and moments in mechanical engineering and neuromuscular connections from biology. All these need to be integrated among other specialties, in order to fully understand human movements.

THE BRANCHES OF MECHANICS

Mechanics is defined as the analysis of forces and their effect. Mechanics also relates to the sciences concerned with the effects of forces acting on objects.

Mechanics may be divided into several branches namely rigid body mechanics, deformable body mechanics, fluid mechanics, relativistic mechanics and quantum mechanics. In

7

rigid body mechanics, objects are assumed to be perfectly rigid. This simplifies the analysis. In deformable body mechanics the deformation of objects is considered. These deformations complicate the analysis. Fluid mechanics is considered with the mechanics of liquid and gases. Relativistic mechanics is considered with Einstein's Theory of Relativity and Quantum Mechanics is considered with Quantum Theory. Each branch of mechanics is best suited for describing and explaining specific features of our physical world.

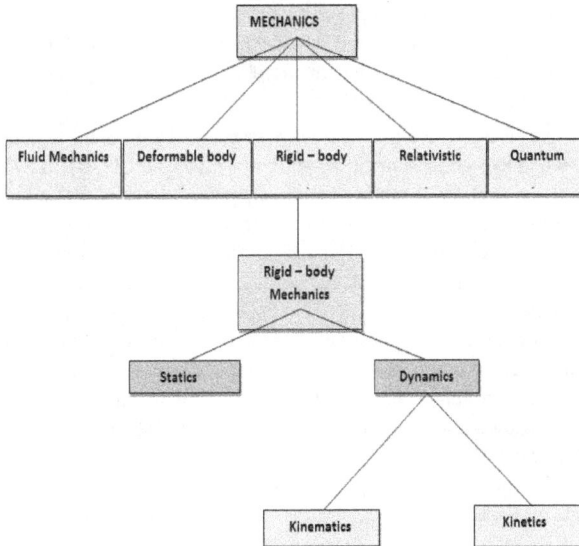

Rigid body mechanics is subdivided into statics and dynamics. Statics is the mechanics of objects at rest or moving at constant velocity and dynamics is the mechanics of objects in accelerated motion. Dynamics is further subdivided into Kinematics and kinetics. Kinematics deals with the description of motion, where as kinetics deals with the force that causes or tends to cause changes in motion.

In this research the researcher made an attempt on kinematic analysis which is the branch of biomechanics concerned with the study of movement with reference to the amount of time taken to carry out the activity and describing the motion of bodies and thus making an attempt through kinematics in finding how far a body moves, how fast it moves and how consistently it moves.

Griffiths (2006) documented that because of the number of interactive disciplines and the large number of variables involved, data collection and analysis in biomechanics is very difficult. But data regarding the mechanics of human movement using motion analysis is a hallmark of the field and integral to the study of motor control and biomechanics.

There are number of ways to collect biomechanical data both in two dimensional (2D) and three dimensional (3D). In two dimensional (2D) analysis, digital video cameras or other convenient method of motion pictures acquisition are used to collect a sequence of still images of the subject, by placing the cameras perpendicular to the plane of the motion to avoid the perspective error. The process of digitization then analysis these images, for information about the human anatomy (i.e. location of hip, knee, etcetera.). Finally, calculation can be performed on this digitization that yield useful biomechanical results – such as angles, distance, displacement, velocity, etcetera (Griffiths, 2006; Bartlett, 2007).

In three dimensional (3D) analysis and motion capture, numerous cameras are used to take image. After two-dimensional information has been captured from each camera, often a technique known as direct linear transform is used to convert the 2D camera data to 3D co-ordinates for a point in space, typically on the anatomy. In both methods, reflective markers are used as "landmarks" that the cameras can use to orient themselves (Griffiths, 2006).

The co-ordinates of this point are then stored on a computer. In order to locate the anatomical landmark to be located, it must be clearly marked on the subject being filmed, so that an accurate identification of the segment end point or joint centre is possible. These co-ordinate data are then smoothed prior to being mathematically manipulated in the calculation of kinematic and kinetic data. Information additional to the co-ordinates of the selected landmarks is required. A large sweep-hand clock may be included in the photographic field to establish the actual frame rate of the camera. Alternatively, internal camera lights which flash at a set rate may be used to mark the film and allow film speed calculation. A spatial scale, such as a large meter rule or cage with known measurement, must also be filmed in the plane of action to convert film scale measures to real values.

KINANTHROPOMETRY

Kinanthropometry is the study of human body size, shape and form and how those characteristics relate to human movement and sporting performance (Eston, 2009). Kinanthropometry is an emerging scientific specialization concerned with the application of measurement to appraise human size, shape, proportion, composition, maturation and gross function. It is a basic discipline for problem-solving in matters related to growth, exercise, performance and nutrition. The area has been defined as the quantitative interface between anatomy and physiology. It puts the individual athlete into objective focus and provides a clear appraisal of his or her structural status at any given time, or more importantly, provides for quantification of differential growth and training influences.

Kinanthropometric measurements relevant to human movement gained formal recognition as a discipline with the inauguration of the International Society for Advancement of Kinanthropometry (ISAK) in 1986. Anthropometrists from all continents have participated in several major multidisciplinary studies that are being or have been conducted to assess the physical characteristics of people. (Ross, Drinkwater, Bailey, Marshall & Leahy, 1980) documented that kinanthropometry is quantitative interface between human structure and function. This interface is examined through the measurement and

10

analysis of age, body size, shape, proportion, composition and maturity as they relate to gross body function. Previous reports have shown that body structure and morphological characteristics are important determinants of performance in many sports and certain physical impressions such as body composition (body fat, body mass, muscle mass) and physique (somatotype) can significantly influence athletic performance (Carter, 1970; Duquet & Carter, 2001). Body composition is an important aspect of fitness (Reilly et al., 1990), and can be predicted from anthropometric measures (Maud & Foster, 1995).

Body fat percentage is a key component of an individual's health and physical fitness profile (Heyward, 1998). It is an important aspect of fitness as superfluous body fat acts as dead weight in activities where body mass must be lifted repeatedly against gravity in movement during exercise (Reilly et al., 1990). A high percentage body fat is detrimental in terms of performance as fat cells are not the primary source of energy production, yet energy is required to move the excess mass around the court (Elliot et al., 1989; Chin et al., 1995). The anthropometrical study reports have shown that body structure and morphological characteristics can determine the selection of participants in many sports. Results of cross-sectional anthropometric studies have tended to suggest that certain physical factors including body composition (body fat, body mass, muscle mass) and physique (somatotype) significantly influence athletic performance (Carter, 1984).

RATIONALE BEHIND SELECTING THE PROBLEM

Modern development in hockey, such as the playing surface, new stick material and interchange of rule, have increased the number of technical demands made on hockey players at all level. Due to modern demands of the game, there is a need of high scientific approach for its performance enhancements.

In India, the studies on biomechanics and kinanthropometric based analysis on penalty corner

11

performance are equivocal. With this point of view the researcher, being a player and qualified coach, is motivated to make an attempt to study biomechanical and kinanthropometric factors on penalty corner push-in and to assess the predominant factors associated with the performance variable.

STATEMENT OF THE PROBLEM

The purpose of the study was to identify the predominant factors in assessing the performance of the penalty corner push-in from the selected biomechanical and kinanthropometric parameters among university hockey players.

HYPOTHESIS

It was hypothesised that performance of the penalty corner push-in might be predicted from selected biomechanical parameters and kinanthropometric characteristics among university level hockey players.

SIGNIFICANCE OF THE STUDY

1. This study would help the physical education teachers and coaches to design a specific programme to identify the talents, which are closely associated with the hockey penalty corner push-in.

2. This study would reveal the influence of biomechanical and kinanthropometric characteristics on the penalty corner push-in of hockey players.

3. This result would be utilized as a screening instrument in analyzing and classifying the best pusher in penalty corner.

DELIMITATIONS

1. This study was delimited only to the university male hockey players whose age ranged between 17 and 28 years.

2. The subjects for the study were taken from Tamil Nadu (67), Karnataka (36) and Kerala (21) state.

3. The study was delimited to the selected variables such as stance width, relative stance width, ball to front foot distance, stick angle, drag distance, drag acceleration, body weight, standing height, arm length, leg length, humerus breadth,

femur breadth, arm girth relaxed, calf girth, skin fold and ball speed.

4. The selected subjects had earlier playing experience of at least three years in hockey.
5. The study was delimited to two dimensional video motion analysis of penalty corner push-in.
6. The study was delimited to penalty corner push-in only in synthetic ground.
7. Casio EX 10 digital video cameras and Max Traq Software was used in the study for the determination of the push-in technique.

LIMITATIONS

1. Certain factors like food habits, life style, climatic condition, social culture, economical status and other environmental factors were not controlled which might influence the performance and these factors were considered as limitations of the study.
2. The differences in playing experience among players due to the participation in tournaments would be considered as a limitation of the study.
3. Similarly the difference in the performance level due to their participation in the coaching programme, if any, would also be added to the limitations.
4. Participants may have performed dynamic cutting movements differently in the experimental setting than they would have during game situation.
5. The accuracy of two dimension kinematics was limited by the manual placement of markers on the surface of the skin over bony landmarks by palpation method.
6. No specific motivational techniques were used to encourage the subjects to attain their maximum performance during testing.

OPERATIONAL DEFINITION

Ball speed – The speed at which the ball was travelling immediately after release from the stick (Kerr & Ness, 2006).

Ball to front foot distance – The distance between the ball and the heel of the front foot at the start of Push-in (Kerr & Ness, 2006).

Biomechanical analysis - This is referred to the analysis of internal and external forces acting on human body in relation to its position by these forces (Griffiths, 2006).

Body weight - Mass is the quantity of matter in the body. Mass is calculated through the measurement of weight, i.e. the force the matter exerts in a standard gravitational field (Michael, 2006).

Circle - The area enclosed by and including the two quarter circles and the lines joining them at each end of the field opposite the centre of the back-lines (FIH, 2013).

Drag acceleration – The acceleration of the ball while in contact with the stick (Kerr & Ness, 2006).

Drag distance – The distance, the ball travels while in contact with the stick (Kerr & Ness, 2006).

Kinanthropometry - Kinanthropometry is the study of human body size, shape and form and how those characteristics relate to human movement and sporting performance (Eston, 2009).

Offence - An action contrary to the Rules which may be penalised by an umpire (FIH, 2013).

Penalty corner (PC) – One of the game situations where defending team is penalized for breach of rule within their own 25m area (Moore, 1993).

Relative stance width – The stance width divided by the height of the player (Kerr & Ness, 2006).

Stance width –The distance between the left and right heel at the start of the push – in (Kerr & Ness, 2006).

Standing height- The perpendicular distance between the Transverse planes of the Vertex and the inferior aspects of the feet (Michael, 2006).

Stick angle - The angle between the stick and ground in the xy plane (Kerr & Ness, 2006).

SUMMARY

Hockey is one of the most popular field games in the world that is being played and watched by both the sexes. A number of scientific studies were taken-up time and again to analyse various factors that contribute to the high level performance of this game. In chapter I, the researcher provided an introduction to the topic of the study and a brief discussion about the factors involved in the study. Then, the description of the problem was provided. Next, the purpose and the objectives of the study were presented. Then, the research hypotheses of the study were presented. These were followed by the delimitations and limitations of the study and the definition of terms used in the study. Finally, the significance of the study was provided.

In chapter - II that follows the study's research framework and a review of literature on the two factors involved in the study is discussed.

METHODOLOGY

Methodology involves the systematic procedure by which the investigator starts from the initial identification of the problem to its final conclusion. The role of the methodology is to carry out the research work in a scientific and valid manner. The purpose of this chapter was to explicate the methodology of this study. This part of the thesis explains the methods adopted in this study which includes selection of subjects, selection and justification of the variables, pilot study, research flow chart, reliability of data, orientation of subjects, administration of tests, research design and statistical methods adopted in this study.

Selection of subjects

The purpose of the study was to predict the performance of the penalty corner push-in from the selected biomechanical and kinanthropometric variables among university hockey players. To achieve the purpose one hundred and twenty four (N=124) male university hockey players were selected purposively from various universities in the states of Tamilnadu, Karnataka and Kerala, South India and their age ranged between 17 and 28 years. The selected subjects had earlier playing experience of at least three years in hockey.

TABLE - 2.1

General Characteristics of University hockey players

Characteristics	Range	Mean(± SD)
Age (years, months)	17.2 - 27.9 years	22.1 (3.1)
Height	1.64 - 1.85 metres	1.73 (0.05)
Weight	60.33 - 86.35 kg	72.49 (7.65)
BMI	18.83 – 31.06 Kg/m^2	24.19 (3.2)

Selection of variables

The present study mainly focus on selected biomechanical and kinanthropometric variables. As far as the performance of penalty corner push-in is concerned following said variables are vital. Similar studies in chapter-2 clearly describe the influences the penalty corner push-in and also it was accorded by the professional experts. After analyzing the various factors associated with performance of the penalty corner push-in, the biomechanical and kinanthropometric characteristics as independent variables were selected for this study. A series of biomechanical variables namely stance width, relative stance width, ball to front foot distance, stick angle, drag distance drag acceleration and the kinanthropometric variables body weight, standing height, arm length, leg length, humerus breadth, femur breadth, arm girth relaxed, calf girth and skin fold were selected. The performance of the penalty corner push-in was selected as dependent variable.

Justification for taking - up the variables

Biomechanical variables

Penalty corner is one of the most important game situations in field hockey with one third of all goals resulting from this tactical situation. **Lopez et al., (2011)** and **Hussain et al., (2011)** reported that biomechanical factor is one of the decisive factors which have been neglected by the Indian researchers. **Kerr & Ness (2006)** recommended that maximizing the front-foot and ball distance will increase the ball speed. **Bari et al., (2014)** reported that stance width plays a significant role in the performance of the push-in. Hence, stance width, relative stance width, ball to front-foot distance, stick angle, drag distance and drag acceleration were selected as biomechanical variables for this investigation.

Kinanthropometric variables

Performance of the Penalty corner push-in is largely depended upon one's kinanthropometric factors. Hence, body weight, standing height, arm length, leg length, humerus breadth, femur breadth, arm girth relaxed, calf girth and skin fold were selected as kinanthropometric parameters for this investigation. **Koley et al., (2012), Sharma et al., (2012), Holway & Seara (2011), Singh et al., (2010), Calo et al., (2009), Keogh et al., (2003), Nieuwenhuis and Spamer & Rossum (2002)** emphasise the importance of kinanthropometric parameters in the penalty corner performance.

Selection of the Test

The investigator selected the following standardized test for testing the selected variables.

TABLE-2.2
SELECTION OF THE TEST

S. No	Variables	Testing equipment / assessment software	Measuring unit
Biomechanical variables			
1	Stance width	Camera Casio EX-10	Metres
2	Relative stance width	Max traq software	Metres
3	Ball to front foot distance		Metres
4	Stick angle		Degree
5	Drag distance		Metres
6	Drag acceleration		Meter/ Sec^2
Kinanthropometric variables			
7	Body weight	Clinical electronic weighing machine	Kg
8	Standing height	Stadiometer	Metres
9	Arm length	Lufkin Anthropometric tape	Centimetres
10	Leg length		
11	Humerus breadth	Small sliding caliper	Centimetres
12	Femer breadth		
13	Arm girth relaxed	Lufkin Anthropometric tape	Centimetres
14	Calf girth		
15	Skin fold	Harpenden skin fold caliper	Millie Metres
Performance variable			
16	Ball speed	Max traq software	Meter/Sec

Research design

A perspective research design was used with performance of the penalty corner push-in in hockey as criterion variable and selected biomechanical and kinanthropometric variables as predictor variables among university level hockey players. The methodology adopted in this study is given through a research flow chart.

18

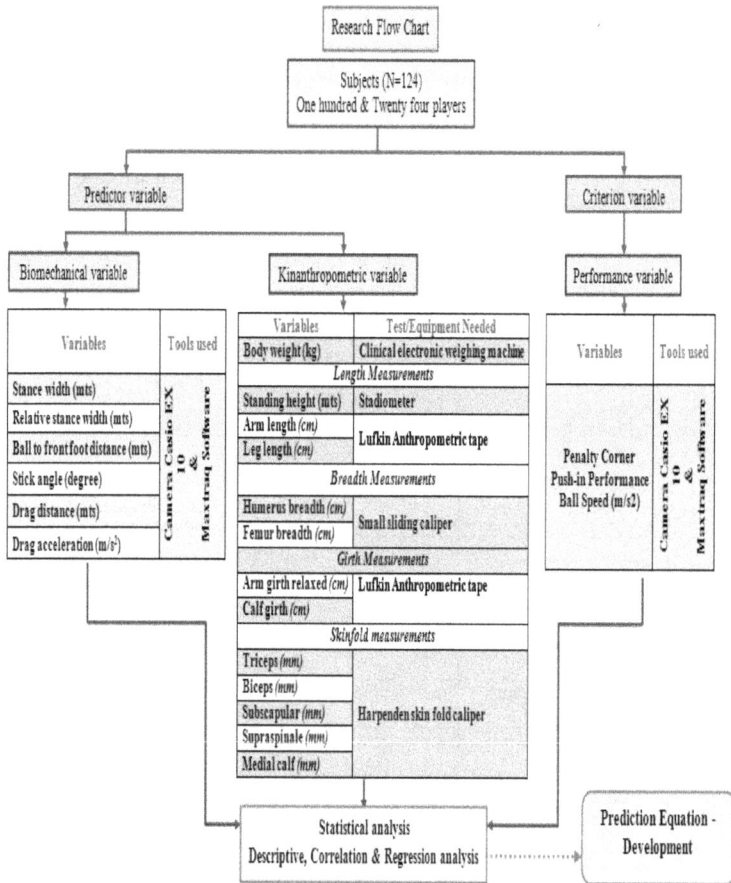

Research Flow Chart

Subjects (N=124)
One hundred & Twenty four players

Predictor variable

Criterion variable

Biomechanical variable

Kinanthropometric variable

Performance variable

Variables	Tools used
Stance width (mts)	Camera Casio EX 10 & Max traq Software
Relative stance width (mts)	
Ball to front foot distance (mts)	
Stick angle (degree)	
Drag distance (mts)	
Drag acceleration (m/s²)	

Variables	Test/Equipment Needed
Body weight (kg)	Clinical electronic weighing machine
Length Measurements	
Standing height (mts)	Stadiometer
Arm length *(cm)*	Lufkin Anthropometric tape
Leg length *(cm)*	
Breadth Measurements	
Humerus breadth *(cm)*	Small sliding caliper
Femur breadth *(cm)*	
Girth Measurements	
Arm girth relaxed *(cm)*	Lufkin Anthropometric tape
Calf girth *(cm)*	
Skinfold measurements	
Triceps *(mm)*	Harpenden skin fold caliper
Biceps *(mm)*	
Subscapular *(mm)*	
Supraspinale *(mm)*	
Medial calf *(mm)*	

Variables	Tools used
Penalty Corner Push-in Performance Ball Speed (m/s2)	Camera Casio EX 10 & Max traq Software

Statistical analysis
Descriptive, Correlation & Regression analysis

Prediction Equation - Development

Pilot Study

Prior to the formal research, a pilot study was conducted in order to tackle the possible hindrance concerning the experimental set-up, camera positions and focus setting. For this purpose, ten male hockey players were filmed while performing penalty corner push-in, with different directions and at different distances. The researcher had ensured optimal location of the camera, correct aperture, focal setting and appropriate lighting. The pilot study paved the way to proceed successfully with the collection of data.

Reliability of data

The reliability of the data was ensured by establishing the subject reliability, tester's reliability and instrumental reliability.

Reliability of the subjects

The subject reliability was established by test and re-test method by using coefficient of correlation for the scores in each of the criterion measures. Re-testing was done within a period of a week from initial tests in each of the criterion measures, to get data for calculating test and re-test coefficient of correlation for reliability of the subjects.

Tester's reliability

The investigator was well versed in the techniques of conducting the test, and had a number of practice sessions in the testing procedures. The standard testing protocol was used to collect biomechanical factors and kinanthropometric measurements by trained and qualified level one anthropometrist of International Society for the Advancement of Kinanthropometry (ISAK). All the measurements were taken by the investigator with the assistance of a person well acquainted with tests and their procedures. Tester competency and reliability of test were established by test-retest methods. A very high correlation was obtained for tester competency in taking measurement and hence the test reliability was accepted.

Instrumental reliability

Clinical electronic weighing machine, Stadiometer, Lufkin anthropometry tape, Campbell Small bone sliding caliper, Harpenden skin fold caliper, Casio EX 10 Camera and Max Traq Software were the standard tools for assessing the intended variables. All instruments were in good condition and workable, purchased in a reputed company. The calibrations were tested and found to be accurate enough to serve the purpose of the study.

Table – 2.3

Reliability co-efficient of the subjects in biomechanical and kinanthropometric by test and re-test methods

S. No	Variables	Co-efficient of Correlation
1	Stance width	0.96*
2	Relative stance width	0.89*
3	Ball to front foot distance	0.93*
4	Stick angle	0.91*
5	Drag distance	0.92*
6	Drag acceleration	0.93*
7	Body weight	0.95*
8	Standing height	0.96*
9	Arm length	0.95*
10	Leg length	0.91*
11	Humerus breadth	0.90*
12	Femur breadth	0.85*
13	Arm girth relaxed	0.87*
14	Calf girth	0.91*
15	Skin fold	0.82*
16	Ball speed	0.92*

* significant at 0.05 level with the table value of 0.63

Orientation of the subjects

The investigator conducted a meeting with the subjects prior to the administration of tests. The purpose, the significance of the study and the requirements of the testing procedures were explained to them in detail, so that there was no ambiguity in their minds, regarding the efforts required from them. All the subjects voluntarily came forward to co-operate in the testing procedures to put in their best efforts in the interest of the scientific investigation and in order to enhance their own performance. The subjects were very enthusiastic and co-operative throughout the project.

Collection of data

The methods of data collected from the university hockey players on selected biomechanical and kinanthropometric variables were explained below. The data were collected as per the schedule given in the table – 2.4

Testing schedule

After obtaining permission from coaches and Directors of Physical Education, the respective team members were contacted and informed about the purpose of the study. Upon receiving consent, test administration dates and times were decided upon. All participants signed the consent form before participation in the study. The testing was done on several phases on a single day and on different venues. Not more than 10 subjects were tested on a single day. The testing was done during the preparatory period of the competition.

TABLE-2.4

Testing Schedule

Session	Administration of Test
Forenoon session	Body weight, Standing height, Arm length, Leg length, Humerus breadth, Femur breadth, Arm girth relaxed, Calf girth and Skin fold
Afternoon session	Video capturing of the penalty corner push-in and variables were measured as a back end work.

Ethical Clearance

The permission for the collecting data from human sample for this research was approved by Institutional Ethics Committee (IEC) for human research of Bharathidasan University (DM/2014/101/42). A copy of the same is in the appendix- III along with the players consent form both in English and Tamil version.

Administration of the Test

Biomechanical Variables

Floor Marking, Camera Set-Up and Video Capturing

A synthetic hockey field was chosen for the conduct of penalty corner push-in test. The film was recorded on sunny and clear weather at synthetic hockey field during evening session. The area of testing in the synthetic hockey field was right quarter of the shooting circle, which is 10m away from the outer edge of the goal post from where the penalty corner push-in is performed.

To acquire biomechanical data, with the assistance of technical experts the high definition camera (Casio EX 10) was used to capture movements of push-in. A cage with the dimensions of 1.0m x1.0m at four control points was used to calibrate the space and it served as a reference point for the measurement of selected biomechanical push-in variables. The camcorder was mounted at the height of one meter and was placed six metres away perpendicular to the trajectory of the ball of the push-in. The shutter speed of the camcorder was adjusted at (1/8000 of a second) in order to eliminate the blurring effects while processing the recordings. A frame rate of 240 frames per second was used. The optical axis of the camera was kept at 90 degree perpendicular to the plane of motion to reduce the perspective error by using Pythagoras theorem (3:4:5 method) and it was checked by plumb line test. After the camera set-up was complete, an object whose dimensions were accurately known was recorded in the plane of motion and was measured in software to ensure the data accuracy.

After a 15-minute standard warm-up session, participants performed the push-in from the right side of the field. Each ball that was pushed within 0.60 Metres on either side of the trapper with maximum ball speed was considered as a successful push-in. Three such successful push-in were recorded. The accurate trial with the greatest ball speed was taken as the best push-in performance for each player. Players were asked to push the ball as fast as they could, as if they were in actual game conditions and the best push-in trial was analysed through the Max traq software.

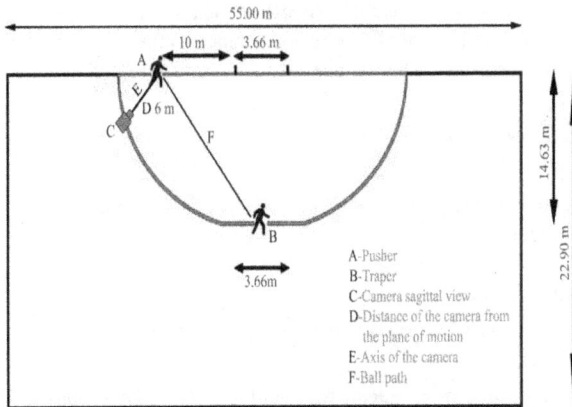

Figure-I Diagram showing the position of the Camera in the Hockey field.

Stance Width

- **Purpose:** To measure the stance width of the subject
- **Equipment & Facilities required:** Max Traq Software, Camera and synthetic hockey field.
- **Procedure:** The stance width of the subjects was calculated using the distance tool in the software. The distance was measured between the left and right heel at the start of the push-in.

24

- **Recording:** The stance width was measured to nearest 0.01 metres.

Relative Stance Width

- **Purpose:** To measure the relative stance width of the subject
- **Equipment & Facilities required:** Max Traq Software, Camera and synthetic hockey field.
- **Procedure:** The relative stance width of the subjects was calculated using the distance tool in the software. The distance was measured between the left and right heel at the start of the push-in. The relative stance width was calculated by using the following formula.

$$\text{Relative Stance width} = \frac{\text{Stance width}}{\text{Height of the subject}}$$

- **Recording:** The relative stance width was measured in nearest 0.01 metres.

Ball to front foot distance

- **Purpose:** To measure the ball to front foot distance of the subject
- **Equipment & Facilities required:** Max Traq Software, Camera and synthetic hockey field.
- **Procedure:** To measure the distance from the ball to the front foot of the subject was calculated using the distance tool in the software. The distance between the ball and the heel of the front foot at the start of Push-in was measured.
- **Recording:** The ball to front foot distance was measured in nearest 0.01 metres.

Stick angle

- **Purpose:** To measure the stick angle of the subject
- **Equipment & Facilities required:** Max Traq Software, Camera and synthetic hockey field.

- **Procedure:** The stick angle of the subjects was calculated using the angle tool in the software. The angle between the stick and ground was measured at the start of push-in.
- **Recording:** The stick angle was recorded in degree.

Drag distance

- **Purpose:** To measure the drag distance of the subject
- **Equipment & Facilities required:** Max Traq Software, Camera and synthetic hockey field.
- **Procedure:** The drag distance of the subjects was calculated using the distance tool in the software. The distance the ball travels while in contact with the stick was measured.
- **Recording:** The drag distance was measured in nearest 0.01 metres.

Drag acceleration

- **Purpose:** To measure the drag acceleration of the subject
- **Equipment & Facilities required:** Max Traq Software, Camera and synthetic hockey field.
- **Procedure:** The drag acceleration of the subjects was calculated using the Max mate software. The ball was digitized while in contact with the stick and it was transformed to max mate software to calculate the drag acceleration.
- **Recording:** The drag acceleration was recorded in metres/sec^2.

Kinanthropometric variables
Body weight

- **Purpose:** To measure the body weight
- **Equipment:** Clinical electronic Weighing Machine
- **Procedure:** The player just stands on the weighing machine with minimal movement with hands by his side. The needle

in the weighing machine should read zero initially. The player stands on the centre of the scales without support and with weight distributed evenly on both feet. Generally the weight in minimal clothing was of sufficient accuracy. Shoes and excess clothing were removed.

- **Recording:** The body weight was recorded in kilograms. The error tolerance as suggested by the international society for the advancement of kinanthropometry (ISAK) norms of 0.5 kg was adopted.

Standing height

- **Purpose:** To measure the standing height of the subject
- **Equipment:** Stadiometer
- **Procedure:** The subject has to stand with the heels together and the heels, buttocks and upper part of the back touching the scale. The head, when placed in the Frankfort plane, need not be touching the scale. The Frankfort plane was achieved when the Orbitale (lower edge of the eye socket) was in the same horizontal plane as the Tragion (notch superior to the tragus of ear). When aligned, the Vertex was the highest point on the skull.

- **Recording:** The standing height was recorded in centimetres. The error tolerance as suggested by the international society for the advancement of kinanthropometry (ISAK) standard of 5 mm was adopted.

Arm length

- **Purpose:** To measure the length of the arm of the subject
- **Equipment:** Lufkin anthropometric tape
- **Procedure:** The subject stands erect to measure the length from the acromion process of the shoulder to the tip of the middle finger. Length from acromion (the most lateral point on the end of the acromial process of the shoulder blade) to radiale (most proximal point on the lateral side of the head of the radius). As the acromion is no part of the humerus, the

27

arm should always be in the same position for exact measuring.

- **Recording:** The arm length was recorded in centimetres. The error tolerance as suggested by the international society for the advancement of kinanthropometry (ISAK) standard of 5 % was adopted.

Leg length

- **Purpose:** To measure the length of the leg of the subject
- **Equipment:** Lufkin anthropometric tape.
- **Procedure:** The subject should stand erect. The measurement can be taken from trochanterion to tibiale laterale, parallel to the longitudinal axis of femur up to the calcanium of the foot, which is base of the foot.
- **Recording:** The leg length was recorded in centimetres. The error tolerance as suggested by the international society for the advancement of kinanthropometry (ISAK) norms of 5 mm was adopted.

Breadth measurement – Humerus breadth

- **Purpose:** To measure the humerus breadth of the subject.
- **Equipment:** Small sliding caliper.
- **Procedure:** The subject assumes a relaxed standing or seated position. The right arm was raised anteriorly to the horizontal and the forearm was flexed at right angles to the arm. The distance between the medial and lateral epicondyles of the humerus was measured. With the small sliding caliper gripped correctly, the middle fingers were used to palpate the epicondyles of the humerus, starting proximal to the sites. The bony points first felt are the epicondyles. The caliper faces are placed on the epicondyles and strong pressure is maintained with the index fingers until the value was read. Because the medial epicondyle is normally lower than the lateral epicondyle the measured distance may be somewhat oblique.

28

- **Recording:** The humerus breadth was recorded in centimetres. The error tolerance as suggested by the international society for the advancement of kinanthropometry (ISAK) standard of 2 mm was adopted.

Femur breadth

- **Purpose:** To measure the femur breadth of the subject.
- **Equipment:** Small sliding caliper.
- **Procedure:** The subject assumes a relaxed seated position with the palms resting on the thighs. The right leg was flexed at the knee to form a right angle with the thigh. The distance was measured between the medial and lateral epicondyles of the femur. With the subject seated and the caliper in place, the middle fingers are used to palpate the epicondyles of the femur beginning proximal to the sites. The bony points first felt were the epicondyles. The caliper faces were placed on the epicondyles and strong pressure is maintained with the index fingers until the value was read.
- **Recording:** The femur breadth was recorded in centimetres. The error tolerance as suggested by the international society for the advancement of kinanthropometry (ISAK) standard of 2 mm was adopted.

Arm girth relaxed

- **Purpose:** To measure the arm girth when subject is in relaxed position.
- **Equipment:** Luffkin anthropometric tape.
- **Procedure:** The subject assumes a relaxed standing position with the arms hanging by the sides. The subject's right arm was abducted slightly to allow the anthropometric tape to be passed around the arm. The measurement was taken snugly around the arm at level midway between the acromion process of scapula and olecranon process of ulna (as marked for triceps and biceps skinfolds). Zero end of the tape was

held in left hand positioned below the other part of the tape held in right hand, so that tape alignment was placed in horizontal plane, parallel to the floor. Apply tension to the tape that fits snugly around the body part but not indent the skin or compress the subcutaneous tissue.

- **Recording:** The arm girth relax was recorded in centimetres. The error tolerance as suggested by the international society for the advancement of kinanthropometry (ISAK) standard of 2 mm was adopted.

Calf girth

- **Purpose:** To measure the circumference of the calf of the subject
- **Equipment:** Luffkin anthropometric tape
- **Procedure:** The subject assumes a relaxed standing position with the arms hanging by the sides. The subject's feet should be separated with the weight evenly distributed. The anthropometrist passes the tape around the calf and then slides the tape up to the correct plane. The stub of the tape and the housing are both held in the right hand while the anthropometrist uses the left hand to adjust the level of the tape to the target level. The anthropometrist resumes control of the stub with the left hand and, using the cross-hand technique, positions the tape so that it is held in a perpendicular plane to the axis of the leg. The tape was then readjusted if necessary to ensure it has not just slipped and does not indent the skin.
- **Recording:** The calf girth was recorded in centimetres. The error tolerance as suggested by the international society for the advancement of kinanthropometry (ISAK) standard of 2 mm was adopted.

Skinfold Measurement –Tricpes

- **Purpose:** To measure the triceps at skinfold site of the subject

- **Equipment:** Harpenden skinfold caliper
- **Procedure:** The subject assumes a relaxed standing position. The right arm should be relaxed with the shoulder joint externally rotated to the mids-prone position and elbow extended by the side of the body. Distance between lateral projection of acromial process and inferior margin of olecranon process was measured on lateral aspect of arm with elbow flexed 90° using a tape measure. Midpoint was marked on lateral side of arm. The near edge of the thumb and finger were in line with the marked site. It should be grasped and lifted (raised) so that a double fold of skin plus underlying subcutaneous adipose tissue was held between the thumb and index finger of the left hand. Fold was lifted 1 cm above marked line on posterior aspect of arm. Caliper was applied 1 cm below fingers.
- **Recording:** The triceps was recorded in millie metres. The error tolerance as suggested by the international society for the advancement of kinanthropometry (ISAK) standard of 5 % was adopted.

Skinfold Measurement - Subscapular

- **Purpose:** To measure the scascapular at skinfold site of the subject
- **Equipment:** Harpenden skinfold caliper
- **Procedure:** The subject assumes a relaxed standing position with the arms hanging by the sides. The line of the skinfold was determined by the natural fold lines of the skin just inferior to inferior angle of scapula. The skinfold measurement was taken with the fold running obliquely downwards at the subscapular skinfold.
- **Recording:** The subscapular was recorded in millie metres. The error tolerance as suggested by the international society for the advancement of kinanthropometry (ISAK) standard of 5 % was adopted.

Skinfold measurement - Biceps

- **Purpose:** To measure the biceps at skinfold site of the subject
- **Equipment:** Harpenden skinfold caliper
- **Procedure:** The subject assumes a relaxed standing position. The right arm should be relaxed with the shoulder externally rotated and the elbow extended by the side of the body. Caliper was applied 1 cm below fingers. Fold was lifted over belly of the biceps brachii at the level marked for the triceps and on line with anterior border of the acromial process and the antecbital fossa. The skinfold measurement was taken parallel to the long axis of the arm at the Biceps skinfold.
- **Recording:** The biceps was recorded in millie metres. The error tolerance as suggested by the international society for the advancement of kinanthropometry (ISAK) standard of 5 % was adopted.

Skinfold measurement – Supraspinale

- **Purpose:** To measure the supraspinale at skinfold site of the subject
- **Equipment:** Harpenden skinfold caliper
- **Procedure:** The subject assumes a relaxed standing position. The right arm should be either abducted or placed across the trunk. Fold was grasped posterior to mid auxiliary line and superiorly to iliac crest along natural cleavage of skin with caliper applied 1 cm below fingers. The skinfold measurement was taken with the fold running obliquely and medially downward at the supraspinale skinfold site.
- **Recording:** The supraspinale was recorded in millie metres. The error tolerance as suggested by the international society for the advancement of kinanthropometry (ISAK) standard of 5 % was adopted.

Skinfold measurement – Medial calf

- **Purpose:** to measure the medial calf skinfold site of the subject
- **Equipment:** Harpenden skinfold Caliper
- **Procedure:** The subject assumes a relaxed standing position with the right foot placed on the box. The right knee was bent at about 90. Fold was lifted at level of maximal calf circumference on medial aspect of calf with knee and hip flexed. The skinfold measurement was taken vertically at the medial calf skinfold site.
- **Recording:** The medial calf was recorded in millie metres. The error tolerance as suggested by ISAK standard of 5 % was adopted

The skin fold measurement was obtained by summing up of triceps, subscapular, biceps, supraspinale and medial calf score.

Ball speed

- **Purpose:** To measure the ball speed in push-in
- **Equipment & Facilities required:** Max Traq Software, Camera and synthetic hockey field.
- **Procedure:** The speed of the ball in push-in was calculated using the max mate software. The ball was digitized while in contact with the stick. The digitized data was saved in the mqa file and it was transformed to max mate software. The ball speed was measured to nearest 0.01 metres immediately after release from the stick.
- **Recording:** The ball speed of the push-in was recorded in metres/sec.

Statistical analysis

Mean and Standard deviations were calculated for each of the selected variables. The inter-relationship among the selected biomechanical, kinanthropometric variables and Penalty corner

33

Push-in ball speed, were computed by using Pearson's product-moment correlation coefficients. The computation of multiple regression was also used. In multiple regression, a criterion variable from a set of predictors was predicted. Step wise argument methods of multiple regression was used in this study to find out the predictor variable that has the highest correlation with the criterion variables which were entered in the equation depending on the contribution of each predictor. The SPSS 15 version package was used to determine the predictive equation.

The prediction formula resulting from multiple regression was basically an extension of the two variables model, $Y = a + bx$. In this research study there were fifteen predictor variables and hence the following statistical regression equation was used. The step wise multiple regression method was used for the selection of variables.

$Y' = a + b_1 x_1 + b_2 x_2 + \ldots b_n x_n$

Where $Y' = Y$ Predictor

a = Constant

b_1, b_2 = Beta weights for predictor variables

X_1, X_2 = predictor variables

Summary

In Chapter – III, the selection of sample, the procedure used for data collection and the different instruments utilized for data collection was also explained. Further, a detailed description of the test administration conducted by the researcher to test the hypotheses of the study was provided. In Chapter – IV that follows, the results of the analysis conducted by the researcher will be presented.

CHAPTER - III

ANALYSIS AND INTERPRETATION OF DATA

➤❧─────────────────────❧◄

The purpose of the study was to identify the dominant factors in assessing the ball speed in push-in from the selected biomechanical and kinanthropometric variables among hockey players. To achieve the purpose of the study, One hundred and twenty four (N=124) male university hockey players were purposively selected from various universities in Tamilnadu, Karnataka and Kerala state from India and their age ranged between 17 and 28 years. The subjects selected had earlier playing experience of at least three years in hockey. To acquire biomechanical data, with the assistance of technical experts the high definition camera (Casio EX 10) was used to capture movements of push-in.

The camcorder was mounted at the height of one meter and was placed six Metres away perpendicular to the trajectory of the ball of the push-in. The shutter speed of the camcorder was adjusted at (1/8000 of a second) in order to eliminate the blurring effects while processing the recordings. A frame rate of 240 frames per second was used. After a 15-minute standard warm-up session, participants performed the push-in from the right side of the field. Each ball that was pushed within 0.60 Metres on either side of the trapper with maximum ball speed was considered as a successful push-in. Three such successful push-in was recorded. The accurate trial with the greatest ball speed was taken as the best push-in performance for each player. Players were asked to push the ball as fast as they could, as if they were in actual game conditions. The kinanthropometric data were collected by following standard testing protocol of

International Society for the Advancement of Kinanthropometry (ISAK).

Descriptive statistics were calculated for each of the selected variables. The inter-relationship among the selected biomechanical, kinanthropometric and performance variables, were computed by using Pearson' product-moment correlation coefficients. All selected biomechanical and kinanthropometric variables that statistically correlated with performance variable were used to form respective linear predictive models (step-wise argument selection).

Analysis of the data

To arrive at meaningful conclusions from the data collected on University male hockey players, analysis were done separately and the results are presented below.

Descriptive analysis

The descriptive statistics – range, minimum, maximum, mean and standard deviation of selected biomechanical and kinanthropometric and ball speed of hockey players are presented in the table – 3.1.

TABLE - 3.1
DESCRIPTIVE STATISTICS OF SELECTED BIOMECHANICAL, KINANTHROPOMETRIC AND PUSH-IN BALL SPEED AMONG HOCKEY PLAYERS

S. No.	Variables	Range	Minimum	Maximum	Mean (N=124)	Std. Deviation (SD ±)
1	Ball speed (m/s)	2.76	15.05	17.81	16.47	0.77
2	Stance width (mts)	0.41	.80	1.21	1.023	0.11
3	Relative stance (mts)	0.22	.47	.69	0.58	0.065
4	Ball to front foot (mts)	0.57	.92	1.49	1.24	0.17
5	Stick angle (degree)	14.32	16.34	30.66	23.99	3.7
6	Drag distance (mts)	0.60	1.20	1.80	1.53	0.16
7	Drag acceleration (m/s^2)	7.15	12.01	19.16	16.08	2.21
8	Height (mts)	0.21	1.64	1.85	1.73	0.056
9	Weight (kg)	26.02	60.33	86.35	72.49	7.65
10	Arm length (cm)	14.52	70.69	85.21	77.83	4.34
11	Leg length (cm)	20.36	87.40	107.76	98.17	6.06
12	Humerus breadth (cm)	1.05	6.30	7.35	6.91	0.31
13	Femur breadth (cm)	1.08	9.11	10.19	9.61	0.32
14	Arm girth relax (mm)	8.37	23.31	31.68	27.48	2.12
15	Calf girth (mm)	8.68	30.41	39.09	34.81	2.55
16	Skin fold (mm)	41.57	34.29	75.86	57.29	10.97

CORRELATION ANALYSIS

The inter-relationship among selected biomechanical, kinanthropometrical and ball speed of Hockey players was computed using Pearson product moment correlation and results are presented in the Table – 4.2.

37

TABLE - 3.2

INTER-CORRELATION OF SELECTED BIOMECHANICAL, KINANTHROPOMETRIC AND PUSH-IN BALL SPEED OF UNIVERSITY HOCKEY PLAYERS

Variable	Ball Speed	Stance Width	Relative stance	Ball to front foot	Stick angle	Drag distance	Drag acceleration	Height	Weight	Arm Length	Leg Length	Humerus breadth	Femur breadth	Arm girth relax	Calf girth	Skin fold
Ball Speed	1	0.277	0.092	-0.075	0.421	0.095	0.257	0.220	0.056	0.378	0.252	-0.332	-0.116	0.207	0.022	0.115
Stance Width		1	0.055	-0.223	0.352	-0.049	0.190	0.104	-0.050	-0.003	-0.013	-0.157	-0.060	-0.006	0.114	0.094
Relative stance			1	-0.059	0.152	-0.073	0.093	0.180	-0.050	0.107	-0.009	-0.053	0.037	0.171	-0.157	-0.169
Ball to front foot				1	0.052	0.095	-0.197	0.122	-0.002	-0.094	-0.113	0.385	0.210	0.084	0.054	-0.111
Stick angle					1	-0.056	0.116	0.127	0.052	0.214	0.168	-0.025	0.046	0.126	0.011	-0.104
Drag distance						1	0.038	-0.027	0.070	-0.271	-0.005	-0.141	0.068	-0.209	0.085	0.047
Drag acceleration							1	0.004	-0.060	0.244	0.147	-0.030	-0.111	0.129	0.008	0.132
Height								1	-0.140	0.141	-0.166	-0.059	-0.273	-0.088	0.112	-0.109
Weight									1	-0.101	-0.109	0.070	0.105	0.176	0.064	-0.074
Arm Length										1	-0.022	-0.117	-0.010	0.038	0.216	0.158
Leg Length											1	-0.068	-0.158	-0.071	-0.238	0.160
Humerus breadth												1	0.144	0.077	-0.098	-0.054
Femur breadth													1	0.171	-0.058	-0.104
Arm girth relax														1	-0.078	0.033
Calf girth															1	-0.066
Skin fold																1

It was evident from the Table – 4.2 that there exist relationships between hockey penalty corner push-in ball speed and stance width, relative stance, ball to front foot, stick angle, drag distance, drag acceleration, height, weight, arm length, Leg length, humerus breadth, femur breadth, arm girth relax, calf girth and skin fold.

The results show that the following biomechanical variables; stance width (r = 0.277), stick angle (r = 0.421) and drag acceleration (r = 0.257), were significantly correlated with the ball speed. The required table 'r' value was 0.184 found at 0.05 level of confidence.

The results show that the following kinanthropometrical variables; height (r = 0.220), arm length (r = 0.378), leg length (r = 0.252) and arm girth relax (r = 0.207) were significantly correlated with the ball speed. The required table 'r' value was 0.184 found at 0.05 level of confidence.

STEP-WISE MULTIPLE REGRESSION ANALYSIS

Stepwise multiple regression was computed to explore the prediction of dominant factors of hockey penalty corner ball speed from the predictor variables of University men hockey players.

The analysis of variance for the influence of predictor variables on Hockey penalty corner ball speed among University men Hockey players is given in table – 3.3

TABLE – 3.3
ANALYSIS OF VARIANCE FOR THE INFLUENCE OF INDEPENDENT
VARIABLES ON PUSH-IN BALL SPEED OF HOCKEY PLAYERS

	Model	Sum of Squares	Df	Mean Square	F	Sig.
1	Regression	13.019	1	13.019	26.225	.000[b]
	Residual	60.567	122	.496		
	Total	73.586	123			
2	Regression	20.635	2	10.318	23.577	.000[c]
	Residual	52.950	121	.438		
	Total	73.586	123			
3	Regression	25.618	3	8.539	21.362	.000[d]
	Residual	47.968	120	.400		
	Total	73.586	123			
4	Regression	28.044	4	7.011	18.320	.000[e]
	Residual	45.541	119	.383		
	Total	73.586	123			
5	Regression	30.791	5	6.158	16.981	.000[f]
	Residual	42.794	118	.363		
	Total	73.586	123			
6	Regression	33.792	6	5.632	16.559	.000[g]
	Residual	39.794	117	.340		
	Total	73.586	123			
7	Regression	36.454	7	5.208	16.269	.000[h]
	Residual	37.132	116	.320		
	Total	73.586	123			
8	Regression	38.303	8	4.788	15.605	.000[i]
	Residual	35.283	115	.307		
	Total	73.586	123			

* - 0.05 level of significance

It was clear from the table – 4.3 that the obtained F value 26.225, 23.577, 21.362, 18.320, 16.981, 16.559, 16.269 and 15.605 respectively are significant at 0.05 level. It reveals that all the independent variables are collectively influenced on the performance ability of Hockey players.

As the F ratio was significant, multiple regression was computed. Multiple regression equation was computed only because the multiple correlations were sufficiently high to warrant prediction from it. Then, the correlation identified the independent variables to be included and their order in the regression equation. Multiple correlations were computed by step-wise argument method and the results are presented in Table –3.4.

TABLE – 3.4
STEP-WISE MULTIPLE REGRESSION BETWEEN PUSH-IN BALL
SPEED AND INDEPENDENT VARIABLES OF HOCKEY PLAYERS

Model	Variables	R	R Square	Adjusted R Square	Std. Error of the Estimate
1	Stick angle	0.421[a]	.177	.170	.70459
2	Humerus breadth	0.530[b]	.280	.269	.66152
3	Arm length	0.590[c]	.348	.332	.63224
4	Leg length	0.617[d]	.381	.360	.61863
5	Arm girth relax	0.647[e]	.418	.394	.60222
6	Drag distance	0.678[f]	.459	.431	.58320
7	Height	0.704[g]	.495	.465	.56578
8	Stance width	0.721[h]	.521	.487	.55390

From Table – 4.4, it was found that the multiple correlations co-efficient for predictors, such as stick angle, humerus breadth, arm length, leg length, arm girth relax, drag distance, height and stance width was 0.721 which produce highest multiple correlations with penalty corner push-in performance. 'R' square values show that the percentage of contribution of predictors to the penalty corner push-in performance (Dependent variables) is in the following order.

1. About 42% of the variation in the performance of the penalty corner push-in was explained by the regression model with one predictor stick angle.
2. About 53% of the variation in the performance of the penalty corner push-in was explained by the regression model with two predictors namely stick angle and humerus breadth. An additional 11% of the variance in the performance of the penalty corner push-in was contributed by humerus breadth.
3. About 59% of the variation in the performance of the penalty corner push-in was explained by the regression model with three predictors namely stick angle, humerus breadth and arm length. An additional 6% of the variance in the

41

performance of the penalty corner push-in was contributed by arm length.

4. About 61% of the variation in the performance of the penalty corner push-in was explained by the regression model with four predictors namely stick angle, humerus breadth, arm length and leg length. An additional 2% of the variance in the performance of the penalty corner push-in was contributed by leg length.

5. About 64% of the variation in the performance of the penalty corner push-in was explained by the regression model with five predictors namely stick angle, humerus breadth, arm length, leg length and arm girth relax. An additional 3% of the variance in the performance of the penalty corner push-in was contributed by arm girth relax.

6. About 67% of the variation in the performance of the penalty corner push-in was explained by the regression model with six predictors namely stick angle, humerus breadth, arm length, leg length, arm girth relax and drag distance. An additional 3% of the variance in the performance of the penalty corner push-in was contributed by drag distance.

7. About 70% of the variation in the performance of the penalty corner push-in was explained by the regression model with seven predictors namely stick angle, humerus breadth, arm length, leg length, arm girth relax, drag distance and height. An additional 3% of the variance in the performance of the penalty corner push-in was contributed by height.

8. About 72% of the variation in the performance of the penalty corner push-in was explained by the regression model with eight predictors namely stick angle, humerus breadth, arm length, leg length, arm girth relax, drag distance, height and stance width. An additional 3% of the variance in the performance of the penalty corner push-in was contributed by stance width.

Percentage of contribution to predictors

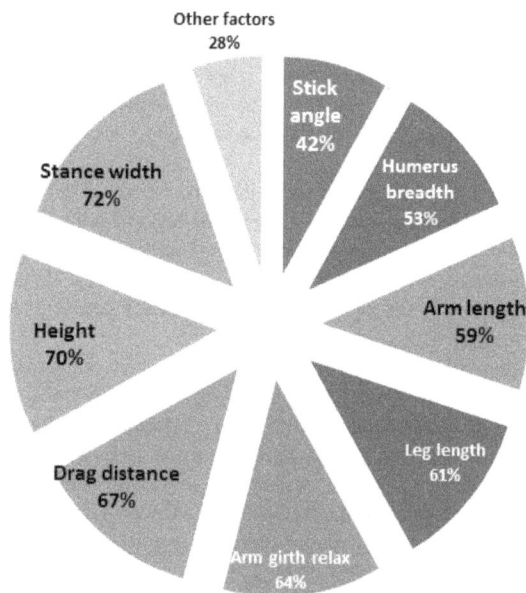

Multiple regression equation was computed and the results are presented in Table – 3.5

TABLE - 3.5
REGRESSION ANALYSIS OF PREDICTION EQUATION OF HOCKEY PLAYERS

Model		Unstandardized Coefficients		Standardized Coefficients	t	Sig.	Collinearity Statistics	
		B	Std. Error	Beta			Tolerance	VIF
Step 1	(Constant)	14.373	.416		34.547	.000		
	Stick angle	.088	.017	.421	5.121	.000	1.000	1.000
Step 2	(Constant)	19.920	1.386		14.375	.000		
	Stick angle	.086	.016	.413	5.349	.000	.999	1.001
	humerus breadth	-.796	.191	-.322	-4.172	.000	.999	1.001
Step 3	(Constant)	15.975	1.733		9.219	.000		
	Stick angle	.074	.016	.356	4.720	.000	.954	1.048
	humerus breadth	-.722	.184	-.292	-3.934	.000	.986	1.014
	Arm length	.048	.014	.268	3.531	.001	.942	1.062
Step 4	(Constant)	13.422	1.976		6.794	.000		
	Stick angle	.067	.016	.323	4.300	.000	.924	1.082
	humerus breadth	-.690	.180	-.279	-3.829	.000	.981	1.019
	Arm length	.050	.013	.281	3.771	.000	.938	1.067
	Leg length	.024	.009	.185	2.518	.013	.963	1.038
Step 5	(Constant)	11.675	2.025		5.765	.000		
	Stick angle	.062	.015	.295	4.005	.000	.907	1.102
	humerus breadth	-.727	.176	-.294	-4.133	.000	.976	1.025
	Arm length	.049	.013	.278	3.832	.000	.937	1.067
	Leg length	.026	.009	.203	2.820	.006	.956	1.046
	Arm girth relax	.071	.026	.196	2.752	.007	.970	1.031
Step 6	(Constant)	8.098	2.301		3.519	.001		
	Stick angle	.060	.015	.288	4.031	.000	.906	1.103
	humerus breadth	-.640	.173	-.259	-3.702	.000	.947	1.056
	Arm length	.061	.013	.341	4.648	.000	.858	1.165
	Leg length	.027	.009	.212	3.039	.003	.954	1.048

	Arm girth relax	.087	.026	.238	3.380	.001	.931	1.075
	Drag distance	1.043	.351	.218	2.970	.004	.860	1.163
Step 7	(Constant)	2.798	2.892		.967	.335		
	Stick angle	.054	.015	.257	3.673	.000	.886	1.129
	humerus breadth	-.614	.168	-.248	-3.659	.000	.945	1.058
	Arm length	.057	.013	.322	4.508	.000	.851	1.175
	Leg length	.032	.009	.252	3.649	.000	.915	1.093
	Arm girth relax	.096	.025	.263	3.821	.000	.916	1.092
	Drag distance	1.069	.341	.223	3.136	.002	.859	1.164
	Height	2.736	.949	.198	2.884	.005	.919	1.088
Step 8	(Constant)	.762	2.950		.258	.797		
	Stick angle	.039	.015	.189	2.557	.012	.761	1.314
	humerus breadth	-.538	.167	-.217	-3.215	.002	.912	1.097
	Arm length	.062	.013	.347	4.905	.000	.834	1.199
	Leg length	.034	.009	.268	3.946	.000	.907	1.103
	Arm girth relax	.100	.025	.274	4.052	.000	.912	1.097
	Drag distance	1.154	.335	.241	3.440	.001	.850	1.176
	Height	2.638	.930	.191	2.837	.005	.917	1.090
	Stance width	1.212	.494	.175	2.455	.016	.823	1.214

From the Table – 4.5, the following regression equations were derived for performance of the penalty corner push-in of the player.

Regression Equation in obtained scores = Push-in Performance ability

Push-in Performance ability = 0.762 + 0.039 (Stick angle) -0.538 (Humerus breadth) +0.062 (Arm length) +0.034 (leg length) + 0.100 (Arm girth relax) +1.15 (Drag distance) +2.63 (Height)+ 1.21 (Stance width).

The regression equation for the penalty corner push-in performance includes stick angle, humerus breadth, arm length, leg length, arm girth relax, drag distance, height and stance width. As the multiple correlations on performance of the penalty corner push-in with the combined effect of these independent variables are highly significant, it is apparent that the obtained regression equation has a high predictive validity.

DISCUSSION ON FINDINGS

In this study, the Biomechnaical variables namely stick angle, drag distance and stance width was found to be significantly correlated with performance of the penalty corner push-in. Kerr & Ness (2006) and Viswanath & Kalidasan (2014) reported that the change in stick angle for the push-in was greater than that of for the push, owing to the differences between the skills. The large change in the angle of the stick during the push-in execution was linearly related to both the drag distance and ball speed of the pusher and recommended that maximizing the stick angle movement during push-in execution led to enhanced overall push-in performance. The results of Kerr & Ness (2006) support the findings of the present study but the minute change in results is due to skill variance of the individuals.

Kerr & Ness (2006); Viswanath & Kalidasan (2014) and McLaughlin (1997) documented that the push-in drag distances generated by the performers was approximately in between the push (0.50 m) and the drag flick (2.18 m). The push-in drag distance was smaller than that used for the drag flick. This is due to the playing rules (International Hockey Federation, 2013) that require the ball to be positioned on the goal line with at least one foot placed outside the field of play at the start of the push-in. The ball cannot be dragged from behind the body as occurs with the drag flick (McLaughlin, 1997). In agreement with drag flick research (McLaughlin, 1997), the distance between the front heel and the ball at the start of the drag correlated positively to ball speed and drag distance for the push-in. It concluded that correct foot placement is vital for maximizing drag distance and ball speed. The push-in technique should, therefore, include maximizing the distance between the front foot and ball at the start of the drag.

Viswanath & Kalidasan (2013) reported that Push-in stance width was highly correlated with the ball speed. Kerr & Ness (2006), observed that for the experienced and inexperienced groups there was little difference to the push-in stance width of between male and females 1.00 m and 0.88 m respectively. But the push-in was smaller than that for the drag flick (McLaughlin, 1997) which is 1.42 m. The experienced group used both larger stance width and relative stance widths than the inexperienced group; therefore, the differences in the stance width between the groups could not be attributed to height variations. The findings of this study were in line with the results of the present study.

When the stance width was broken down, it was found that, as the ball-front foot distance increased so too did the ball speed (Kerr & Ness, 2006). Thus, for a given stance width the distance between the ball and front heel should be maximized so as to maximize drag distance. This, in turn, allows a greater distance over which to accumulate speed.

In this study, the kinanthropometric variables namely, humerus breadth, arm length, leg length, arm girth relax and height was found to be significantly correlated with penalty corner push-in. Among the breadth measurements the humerus breadth was found to be significantly correlated with penalty corner push-in performance. The findings of the present study had strong agreement with the findings of (Viswanath & Kalidasan, 2014). Since it is a variable which values the diameter of the bone and relates to the lever at the time of making the movement of skills and push, this movement is important for increasing the speed during the push-in.

Viswanath & Kalidasan (2014) viewed that arm length and leg length is directly proportional to the stance width and drag distance. If the leg length and arm length increases, stance width and drag distance also increase which in turn makes the

47

speed of the ball also to increase for effective execution of the push-in.

Among the girth measurements arm girth relax was found be the best predictor for penalty corner push-in performance. Beneath the skin is a layer of substance fat and the percentage of total body fat can be measured by taking the girth measurements. The average girth measures helps in developing strength as well as its associated factors which helps to maintain the optimum performance (Viswanath & Kalidasan, 2014). The result reveals that the height was the best predictor for penalty corner push-in performance. Kinanthropometric factors can influence the effectiveness of such responses, as it has been observed in other sports. In this research, the investigator presented the results with reference to the kinanthropometric characteristics contributing to the penalty corner push-in performance in terms of predictive equation. If the height increases, stance width of the pusher increases for the successful push-in execution.

It was registered that the pusher would execute the push-in task with greater accuracy due to regular practice of the skill (Kerr & Ness, 2006; Viswanath & Kalidasan, 2014). The findings of the present study had strong agreement with the findings of (Kerr & Ness, 2006) that 0.6 m accuracy allowance on either side of the trapper may have been too easy to obtain. Compared to previous research, the push-in ball speeds were faster than the push (10.6 m/s) but slower than the drag flick (21.9 m/s) (McLaughlin, 1997), the slap shot (25.3 m/s) and the hit (38.6 m/s). The faster ball speeds for the hit and the slap shot were expected because they incorporated a back swing before ball contact to generate additional speed transfer from the stick to the ball. The push and drag flick skills, however, do not involve a back swing for speed contributions.

DISCUSSION ON HYPOTHESIS

It was hypothesised that penalty corner push-in performance might be predicted from selected biomechanical parameters and kinanthropometric characteristics among university hockey players.

The findings of the results reveal that stick angle, humerus breadth, arm length, leg length, arm girth relax, drag distance, height and stance width were selected predictors for penalty corner push-in ball speed. Hence the researcher's hypothesis was partially accepted.

CHAPTER - IV

SUMMARY, CONCLUSIONS AND RECOMMENDATIONS

4.1 SUMMARY

In current scenario, the nature of sports and games has gone through tremendous radical changes in international arena, due to advancement of sports sciences. Biomechanics one of the branches of sports sciences, is the study of the mechanics of living things. It demands knowledge of both biology and various branches of physics and engineering which comprises mechanics. Kinanthropometry another sports science subject which has been defined as the quantitative measurement and analysis of age, body, size, shape, proportion, composition and maturation as they relate to gross body function.

In modern hockey, there is increase in the number of set plays performed during the game. The penalty corner is one of the most important tactical situations in field hockey. The penalty corner in hockey was first introduced in 1908. Penalty corner is awarded for foul committed by the defending team in its own entire 23 meters area. Depending upon the nature of foul penalty corner is awarded. With penalty corner one has greater scoring opportunities, because at the time of start of penalty corner only five defenders will be permitted within the circle, behind the goal line but all the attackers are permitted to stand just outside the circle.

The champions of today are seen perfect in the conversion of penalty corners. Penalty corner execution can be separated into three progressive phases: the push-in, the trap and the strike. The push starts with an attacker standing close to the goal line with at least one foot outside the field of play. The left shoulder points in the direction of the push. The hook of the

50

stick rests against the ball. The push-in movement involve a rapid rotation of the hip, shoulders and arms in the direction of the trapper while the body weight is being transferred from the back foot to the front foot. The ball is dragged or pushed over the playing surface by the Hockey stick for some distance and then released in the direction of the trapper. In the artificial surface dragging action is used frequently. The trap phase follows when the ball reaches the top of the circle and is trapped by another attacking player just outside the circle. The trapper propels the ball back into the circle for the phase three to commence, the phase three consists of a third attacker striking the moving ball towards the goal or another attacking player.

Few researchers have focused on penalty corner push-in techniques in Indian field hockey. Push-in part in penalty corner plays critical role in conversion of penalty corner. If push-in is with great speed, the striker has extra time before defender reaches the penalty circle.

Modern development in hockey, such as the playing surface, new stick material and change of rules, have increased the number of technical demands made on hockey players at all levels. Due to modern demands of the game, there is a need of high scientific approach for its performance enhancements.

In India, the studies on biomechanics and kinanthropometric based analysis on penalty corner performance are equivocal. With this point of view the researcher, being a player and qualified coach, is motivated to make an attempt to study biomechanical and kinanthropometric factors on penalty corner push-in and to assess the predominant factors associated with the performance variable.

To achieve the purpose of the study, one hundred and twenty four (N=124) male university hockey players were purposively selected from various universities in Tamilnadu, Karnataka and Kerala states from India and their age ranged between 17 and 28 years. The subjects selected had earlier playing experience of at least three years in hockey. To acquire biomechanical data, with the assistance of technical experts the high definition camera (Casio EX 10) was used to capture.

Stance width, relative stance width, ball to front foot distance, stick angle, drag distance, drag acceleration, body weight, standing height, arm length, leg length, humerus breadth, femur breadth, arm girth relaxed, calf girth, skin fold and ball speed were selected as variables as they may have direct relation to the performance of penalty corner push-in in competitive situation.

A series of biomechanical components were assessed by standardised equipments namely Casio EX 10 camera and Max traq software following standardised testing protocol. The kinanthropometric parameters were assessed by standardized testing instruments namely clinical electronic weighing machine, stadiometer, lufkin anthropometric tape, small sliding calliper and harpenden skin fold calliper by following standard testing protocol of International society for the advancement of kinanthropometry and ball speed was assessed by Max traq software.

The camcorder was mounted at the height of one meter, placed 6 meters away perpendicular to the trajectory of the ball of the push-in. The shutter speed of the camcorder was adjusted at (1/8000 of a second) in order to eliminate the blurring effects while processing the recordings and with a frame rate of 240 frames per second was used. A cage with the dimensions of 1.0x1.0m at 4 control points was used to calibrate the space, in which the push-in was performed. After a 15-minute standard warm-up session, participants perform the push-in from the right side of the field, three successful push-in was recorded that is within 0.60 m each side of the trapper were performed. The accurate trial with the greatest ball speed was deemed as the best push-in trial for each player. Players were asked to push the ball as fast as they could, as if they were in actual game conditions and the best push-in trial was analysed through the Max traq software. The kinanthropometric data were collected by following standard testing protocol of International Society for the Advancement of Kinanthropometry (ISAK).

Mean and standard deviations were calculated for each of the selected variables. The inter-relationship among the selected biomechanical, kinanthropometric and ball speed, were computed by using Pearson Product-Moment Correlation Coefficients. The computation of multiple regression was also used. In multiple regressions, a criterion variable from a set of predictors was predicted. Step-wise argument methods of multiple regression was used in this study to find out the predictor variable that has the highest correlation with the criterion variables were entered in the equation depending on the contribution of each predictor variables.

The constant 'a' obtained for the regression equation was 0.762. The beta weights for the eight selected variables were 0.039 for stick angle, -0.538 for humerus breadth, 0.062 for arm length, 0.034 for leg length, 0.100 for arm girth relax, 1.15 for drag distance, 2.63 for height and 1.21 for stance width. Thus, the equation for predicting dominant factors of ball speed of the Inter University Hockey players were obtained and was and given as:

Push-in Performance ability = 0.762 + 0.039 (Stick angle) -0.538 (Humerus breadth) + 0.062 (Arm length) + 0.034 (leg length) + 0.100 (Arm girth relax) +1.15 (Drag distance) +2.63 (Height) + 1.21 (Stance width).

4.2 Conclusions

From the analysis of data, the following conclusions were drawn.

1. The results revealed that there was inter-relationship exist between performance of the penalty corner push-in and selected biomechanical and kinanthropometric variables.
2. The biomechanical variables namely stick angle, drag distance and stance width along with the kinanthropometric variables namely humerus breadth, arm length, leg length, arm girth relax and height were the common predominant

53

variables for predicting the performance variable of university hockey players.

4.3 Recommendations

Recommendations for implications

1. Coaches in the game of hockey should give due importance to predominance factors during the selection process / talent identification process which is the key factor for penalty corner push-in performance.
2. Including biomechanicst in the team of officials with the hockey team.

Recommendations for further study

1. Similar quantifying and profiling studies may be undertaken with hockey players of different levels such as state and national levels.
2. Similar project may be undertaken with hockey players with three dimensional analysis.
3. Related study may be conducted on women hockey players.
4. Similar study may also be conducted on different games and sports.

BIBLIOGRAPHY

❖ Ackland, T. R., Elliott, B., & Bloomfield, J. (Eds.). (2009). Applied anatomy and biomechanics in sport. Human Kinetics.

❖ Ansari, N. W., Bari, M. A., Hussain, I., & Ahmad, F. (2014). Three dimensional kinematic analysis of the drag flick for accuracy. *International Journal of Applied Sciences and Engineering Research, 3*(2), 431-435.

❖ Bari, M. A., Ansari, N. W., Ahmad, F., & Hussain, I. (2014). Three dimensional analysis of drag-flick in the Field Hockey of University players. *Advances in Physics Theories and Applications, 29*, 87-93.

❖ Bari, M. A., Ansari, N. W., Hussain, I., Ahmad, F., & Khan, M. A. (2014).Three dimensional analysis of variation between successful and unsuccessful drag flick techniques in Field Hockey. *International journal of Research studies in Science, Engineering and Technology, 1*(2), 74-78.

❖ Bartlett, R. (2007). *Introduction to sports biomechanics: Analysing human movement patterns.* Routledge.

❖ Bretigny, P., Leroy, D., Button, C., Chollet, D., & Seifert, L. (2011). Coordination profiles of the expert field hockey drive according to field roles. *Sports Biomechanics,* 10(4), 339-350.

❖ Calo, C. M., Sanna, S., Piras, I. S., Pavan, P., & Vona, G. (2009). Body composition of Italian female hockey players. *Biology of Sport, 26*(1), 23.

❖ Carter, (1984). Somatotypes of Olympic athletes. In: Carter, J., E., L. (ed.) Physical Structure of Olympic Athletes. Part II: Kinanthropometry of Olympic Athletes. Karger, Basel, pp. 80-109.

❖ Carter, J., E., L. (1970). The somatotypes of athletes-a review. *Hum.Biol.* 42:535-569.

❖ Cetin, E., Ozdemir, O., & Ozdol, Y. (2014). Kinematic analysis last four stride lengths of two different long jump performance. *Procedia-Social and Behavioral Sciences, 116,* 2747-2751.

❖ Chin, M.; Wong, A.S.K.; So, R.C.H.; Siu, O.T.; Steininger, K. and Lo, D.T.L. (1995). Sport specific testing of elite badminton players. Britis Journal of Sports Medicine, 29(3):153 - 157.

❖ Chivers, L., and Elliott, B. (1987). The penalty corner in field hockey. *Excel,* 4, 16.

❖ Chris Moore,(1993). *No Change for the sake of the change,* world Hockey, p.111.

❖ Duquet, W., & Carter, J., E., L. (2001). Somatotyping. In: R.Eston and T.Reilly (eds.) Kinanthropometry and Exercise Physiology Laboratory Manual. Vol. 1: Anthropometry. Routledge, London, pp. 47-64.

❖ Elliot, B.C.; Ackland, T.R.; Blanksby, B.A.; Hood, K.P. and Bloomfield, J. (1989). Profiling junior tennis players part 1 : morphological, Physiological and psychological normative data. Australian Journal of Science and Medicine in Sport, 21(3):14 – 21

❖ Eston, Roger & Reilly, Thomas (2009). *Kinanthropometry and exercise physiology laboratory manual. Test procedures and data.* USA: Routledge.

❖ Gomez, M., López De Subijana, C., Antonio, R., & Navarro, E. (2012). Kinematic pattern of the drag-flick: a case study. *Journal of human kinetics, 35*(1), 27-33.

❖ Gorman, A. J. (2013). *The timing and magnitude of muscular activity patterns during a field hockey hit* (Doctoral dissertation, University of Lincoln).

❖ Green, A. (2014). The biomechanical and physiological predictors of golf drive performance, before and after a hole-to-hole distance walk (Doctoral dissertation)

❖ Griffiths. W. Iwan (2006). *Principles of Biomechanics & Motion analysis.* Lippincott Williams & Wilkins

❖ Heyward, V. H. (1998). Advanced Fitness Assessment and Exercise Prescription. Champaign, Illinios: Human Kinetics.

❖ Holway, F. E., & Seara, M. (2011). Kinanthropometry of world champion junior male field hockey players. *Apunts. Medicina de l'Esport, 46*(172), 163-168.

❖ Hong, Y. (Ed.). (2012). International research in sports biomechanics. Routledge.

❖ Horan, S. A., Evans, K., Morris, N. R., & Kavanagh, J. J. (2014). Swing kinematics of male and female skilled golfers following prolonged putting practice. Journal of sports sciences, 32(9), 810-816.

❖ Hussain, I., Mohammad, A., Khan, A., Bari, M. A., Ahmad, A., & Ahmad, S. (2011). Penalty stroke in field hockey: A biomechanical study. *International journal of sports science and engineering, 5*(1), 53-57.

❖ Johnson, D., & McPhee, J. (2014). Predictive Dynamic Simulation of the Golf Swing, Including Golfer Biomechanics and Distributed Flexibility in the Shaft. Procedia Engineering, 72, 799-804.

❖ Kapidzic, A., Huremovic, T., Biberovic, A., Mehinovic, J., Selimovic, A., & Smajic, M. (2014). Kinematic analysis forearm passing in volleyball at different distances. *Journal of Education and Practice, 5*(10), 75-84.

❖ Keogh, J. W., Weber, C. L., & Dalton, C. T. (2003). Evaluation of anthropometric, physiological, and skill-related tests for talent identification in female field hockey. *Canadian Journal of Applied Physiology, 28*(3), 397-409.

❖ Kerr, R., & Ness, K. (2006). Kinematics of the field hockey penalty corner push-in. *Sports Biomechanics, 5*(1), 47-61.

❖ Kerr, R., and Ness, K. (2002). A three-dimensional kinematic analysis of the field hockey penalty corner push-in. *Proceedings of the Australian Conference of Science and*

Medicine in Sport: sports medicine and science at the extremes *5*(4), p. 12.

❖ Knudson, D. (2007). *Fundamentals of biomechanics*. Springer.

❖ Koley, S., & Vashisth, D. (2014). Correlations of back endurance with anthropometric variables and performance test in Indian elite male hockey players. *Human Biology Review*, *3*(2), 175-183.

❖ Koley, S., Jha, S., & Sandhu, J. S. (2012). Study of back strength and its association with selected anthropometric and physical fitness variables in inter-university Hockey players. *Anthropologist*, *14*(4), 359-363.

❖ Laird, P., and Sutherland, P. (2003). Penalty corners in field hockey: A guide to success. International Journal of Performance Analysis in Sport, 3 (1), 19–26.

❖ Lopez de Subijana Hernández, C., Juarez Santos-Garcia, D., & Navarro Cabello, E. (2011). The application of biomechanics to penalty corner drag-flick training: a case of Study. *Journal of Sports Science and Medicine*, *11*, 590-595.

❖ Lopez De Subijana, C., Juárez, D., Mallo, J., & Navarro, E. (2010). Biomechanical analysis of the penalty-corner drag-flick of elite male and female hockey players. *Sports Biomechanics*, *9*(2), 72-78.

❖ Maud, P. J. and Foster, C. (1995).Physiological Assessment of Human Fitness. Champaign, Illinios: Human Kinetics.

❖ McErlain, Naylor, S., King, M., & Pain, M. T. G. (2014). Determinants of countermovement jump performance: a kinetic and kinematic analysis. *Journal of sports sciences*, *32*(15), 1-8.

❖ McGinnis, P. (2005). Biomechanics of sport and exercise. Human Kinetics.

❖ Michael Marfell – Jones, Tim Olds, Arthur Stewart and Lindasy Carter (2006). International Standards for Anthropometric Assessment. International Society for Advancement of Kinanthropometry. P:58.

❖ Michaud, Paquette, Y., Magee, P., Pearsall, D., & Turcotte, R. (2011). Whole-body predictors of wrist shot accuracy in ice hockey: a kinematic analysis. *Sports Biomechanics*, *10*(01), 12-21.

❖ Michaud, Paquette, Y., Pearsall, D. J., & Turcotte, R. A. (2009). Predictors of scoring accuracy: ice hockey wrist shot mechanics. *Sports Engineering*, *11*(2), 75-84

❖ Morrison, A., McGrath, D., & Wallace, E. (2014). Changes in club head trajectory and planarity throughout the golf swing. *Procedia Engineering*, *72*, 144-149.

❖ Nieuwenhuis, C. F., Spamer, E. J., & Rossum, J. H. V. (2002). Prediction function for identifying talent in 14-to 15-year-old female field hockey players. *High Ability Studies*, *13*(1), 21-33.

❖ Nordin, M., & Frankel, V. H. (Eds.). (2001). *Basic biomechanics of the musculoskeletal system*. Lippincott Williams & Wilkins.

❖ Orth, D., Davids, K., Araújo, D., Renshaw, I., & Passos, P. (2014). Effects of a defender on run-up velocity and ball speed when crossing a football. *European journal of sport science*, *14*(1), S316-S323.

❖ Pactrick McLaughlin (1997). Three dimensional biomechanical analysis of the hockey drag flick. National sports research centre. Australia.

❖ Pineiro, R., Sampedro, J., and Refoyo, I. (2008). Differences between international men's and women's teams in the strategic action of the penalty corner in field hockey. International Journal of Performance Analysis in Sport, 7 (3), 67–83.

❖ Reilly, T.; Secher, N.; Snell, P. and Williams, C. (1990). Physiology of Sports. London: E. & F.N. SPON

❖ Ross, W.D., Drinkwater, D.T., Bailey, D.A., Marshall, G.R., & Leahy, R.M. (1980). Kinanthropometry; Traditions and new perspective. In: M.Ostyn.

❖ Rules of Hockey. (2013). Switzerland: International Hockey Fedeartion.

❖ Sharma, A., Tripathi, V., & Koley, S. (2012). Correlations of anthropometric characteristics with physical fitness tests in Indian professional hockey players. *Journal of Human Sport & Exercise, 7*(3), 698-705.

❖ Sim, T., Jang, D. J., & Oh, E. (2014). A methodological approach for the biomechanical cause analysis of golf-related lumbar spine injuries. Computer methods in biomechanics and biomedical engineering, 17(16), 1801-1808.

❖ Sinclair, J., Currigan, G., Fewtrell, D. J., & Taylor, P. J. (2014). Biomechanical correlates of club-head velocity during the golf swing. *International Journal of Performance Analysis in Sport, 14*(1), 54-63.

❖ Sinclair, J., Fewtrell, D., Taylor, P. J., Bottoms, L., Atkins, S., & Hobbs, S. J. (2014). Three-dimensional kinematic correlates of ball velocity during maximal instep soccer kicking in males. *European journal of sport science*, 1-7.

❖ Singh, M., Singh, M. K., & Singh, K. (2010). Anthropometric measurements, body composition and physical parameters of Indian, Pakistani and Sri Lankan field hockey players. *Serbian journal of sports sciences, 4*(2), 47-52.

❖ Sommer, M., Häger, C., & Rönnqvist, L. (2014). Synchronized metronome training induces changes in the kinematic properties of the golf swing. Sports Biomechanics, 13(1), 1-16.

❖ Subijana, de, C. L., Gomez, M., Martin-Casado, L., & Navarro, E. (2012). Training-induced changes in drag-flick technique in female field hockey players. *Biology of Sport, 29*(4), 263.

❖ Subijana, de, C. L., Juarez, D., Mallo, J., & Navarro, E. (2011). The application of biomechanics to penalty corner drag-flick training: a case study. *Journal of sports science & medicine, 10*(3), 590.

❖ Takeda, T., Itoi, O., Takagi, H., & Tsubakimoto, S. (2014). Kinematic analysis of the backstroke start: differences between backstroke specialists and non-specialists. *Journal of sports sciences, 32*(7), 635-641.

60

❖ Vinson, D., Padley, S., Croad, A., Jeffreys, M., Brady, A., & James, D. (2013). Penalty corner routines in elite women's indoor field hockey: Prediction of outcomes based on tactical decisions. *Journal of sports sciences*, 31(8), 887-893.

❖ Viswanath and kalidasan (2012) Selected biomechanical and kinanthropometrical factors in relation to penalty corner performance in field hockey. *ISBS conference proceedings*, Taiwan.

❖ Viswanath,S & Kalidasan, R. (2014). Analysis of kinanthropometric characteristics and push-in ball speed in hockey. *Star Research Journal*, 6(2), 6-9.

❖ Viswanath,S & Kalidasan, R. (2014). Biomechanical analysis of penalty corner push-in. *International Journal of Scientific Research*, 3(6), 35-36.

❖ Wein, Horst. (1981). *The advance science of hockey*. (p. 20). London: Pelham Books Ltd.

❖ Willmott, A. P. (2010). *The dynamics of the stick motion in the field hockey hit*. (Doctoral dissertation, Indiana University).

❖ Wong, F. K., Keung, J. H., Lau, N. M., Ng, D. K., Chung, J. W., & Chow, D. H. (2014). Effects of body mass index and full body kinematics on tennis serve speed. *Journal of Human Kinetics*, 40(1), 21-28.

www.ingramcontent.com/pod-product-compliance
Lightning Source LLC
Chambersburg PA
CBHW021222020426
42331CB00003B/433